Ric and Run!

By Raffi Rap
Illustrated by John Nez

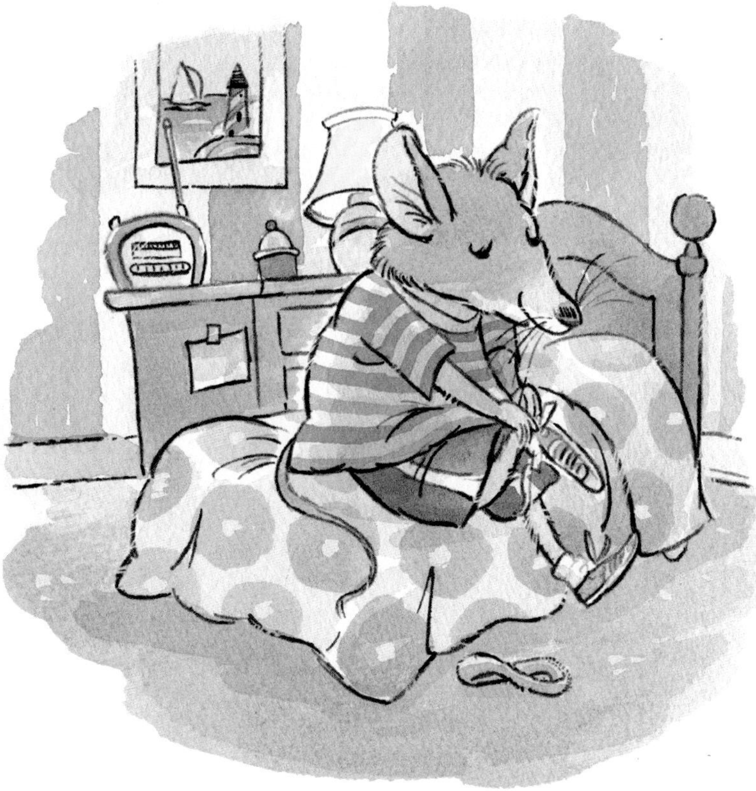

Target Skill Consonant *Rr*/r/

PEARSON
Scott Foresman

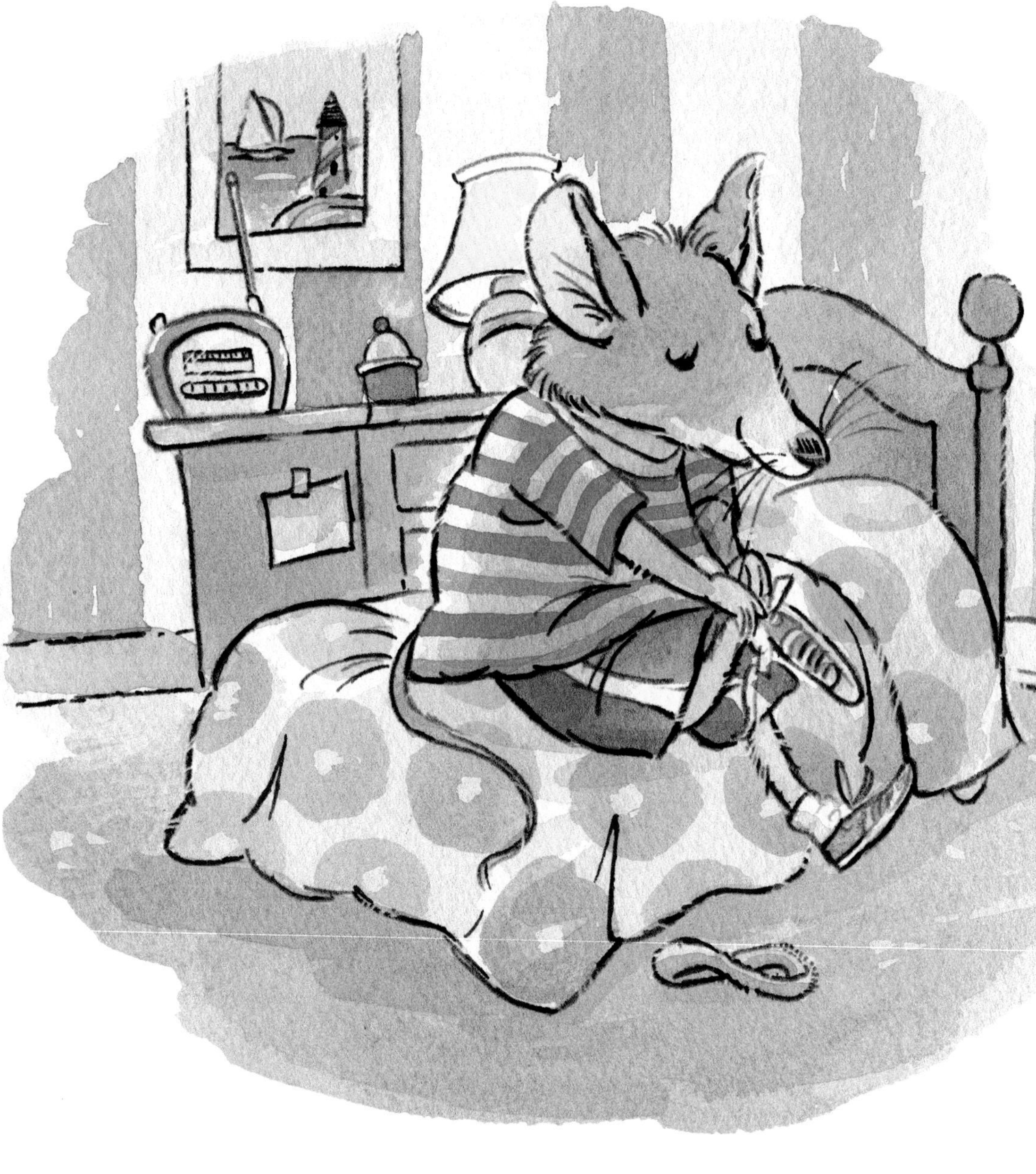

Ric is a rat.

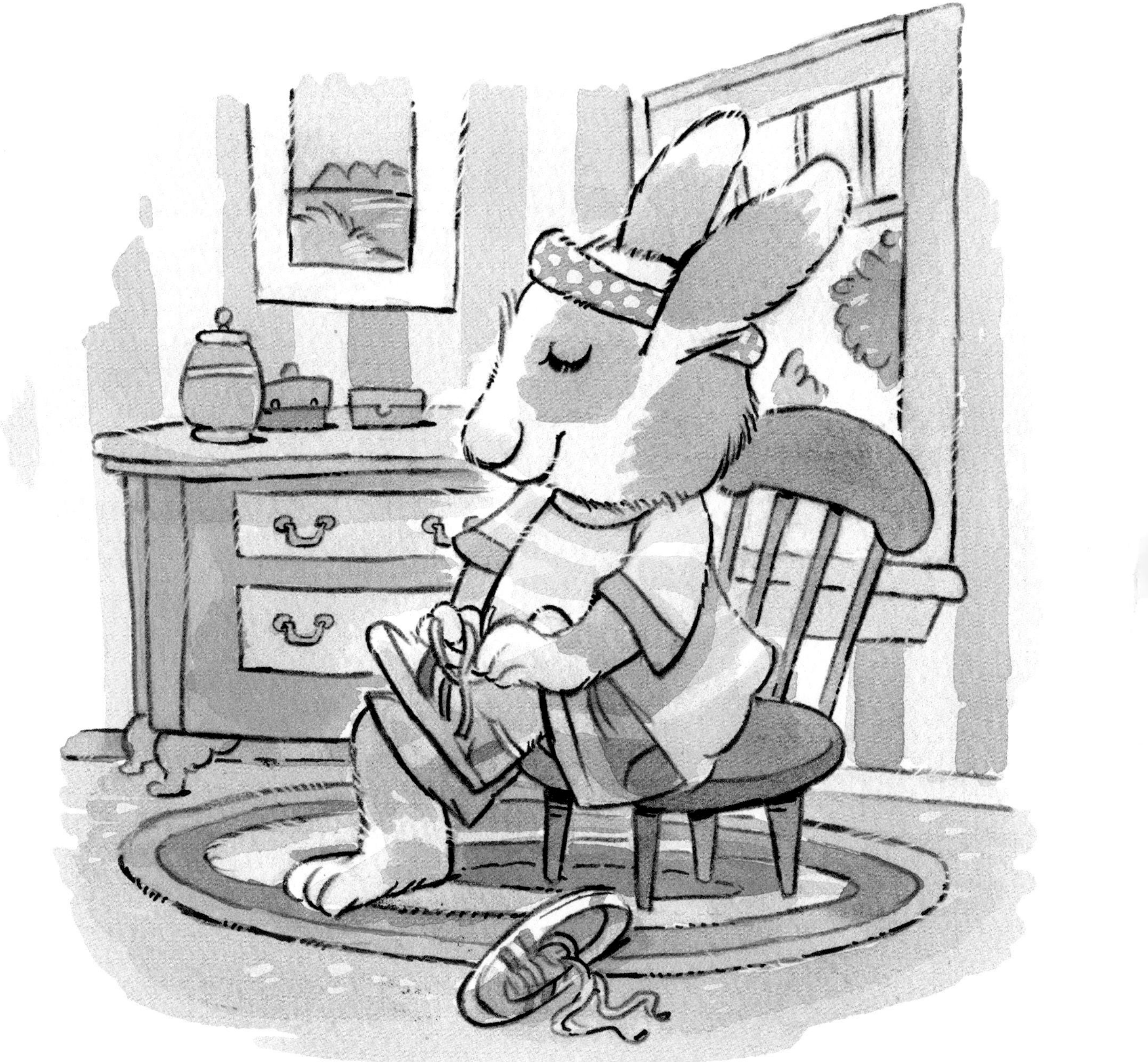

Is Rin a rat?

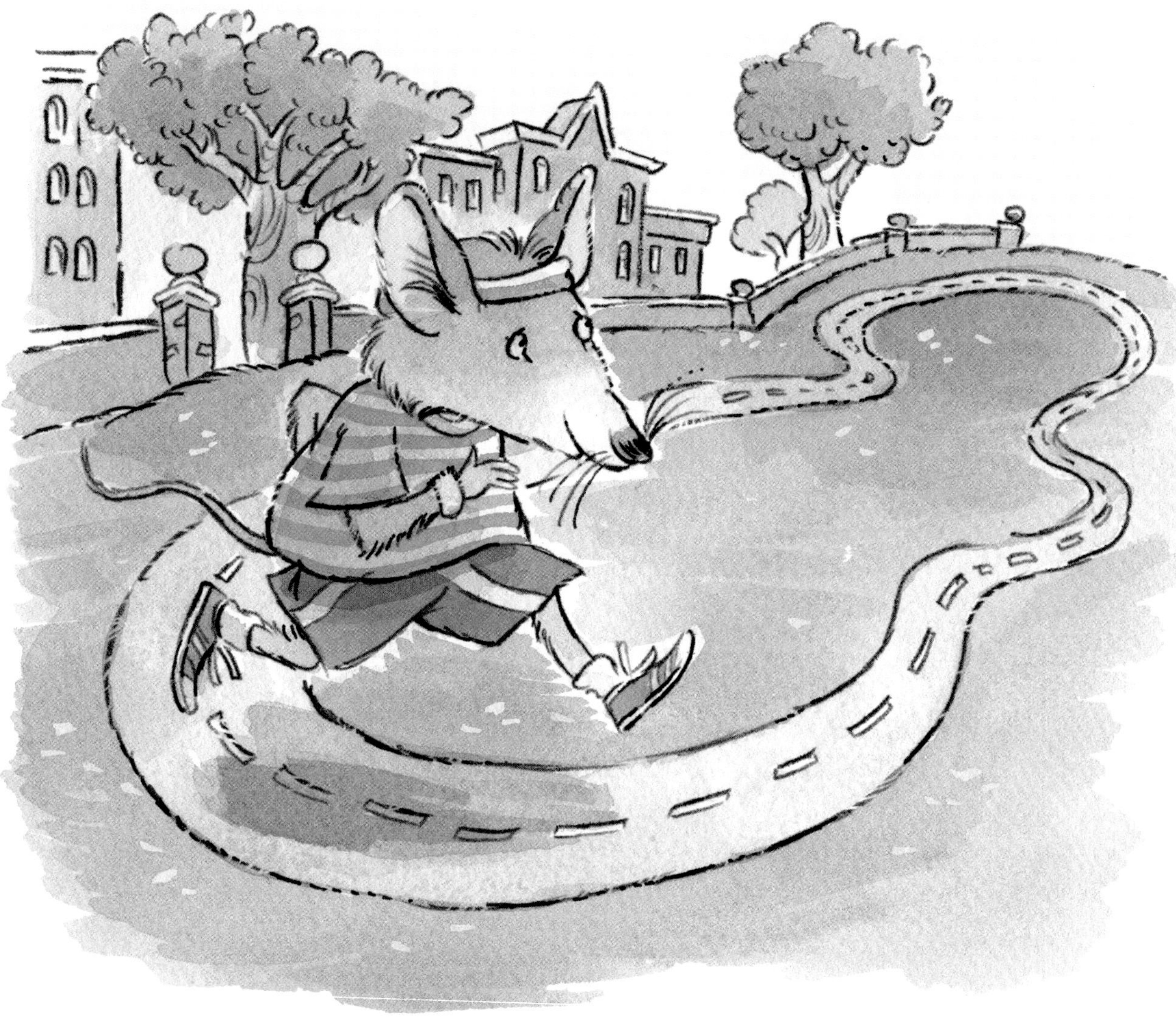

He ran!

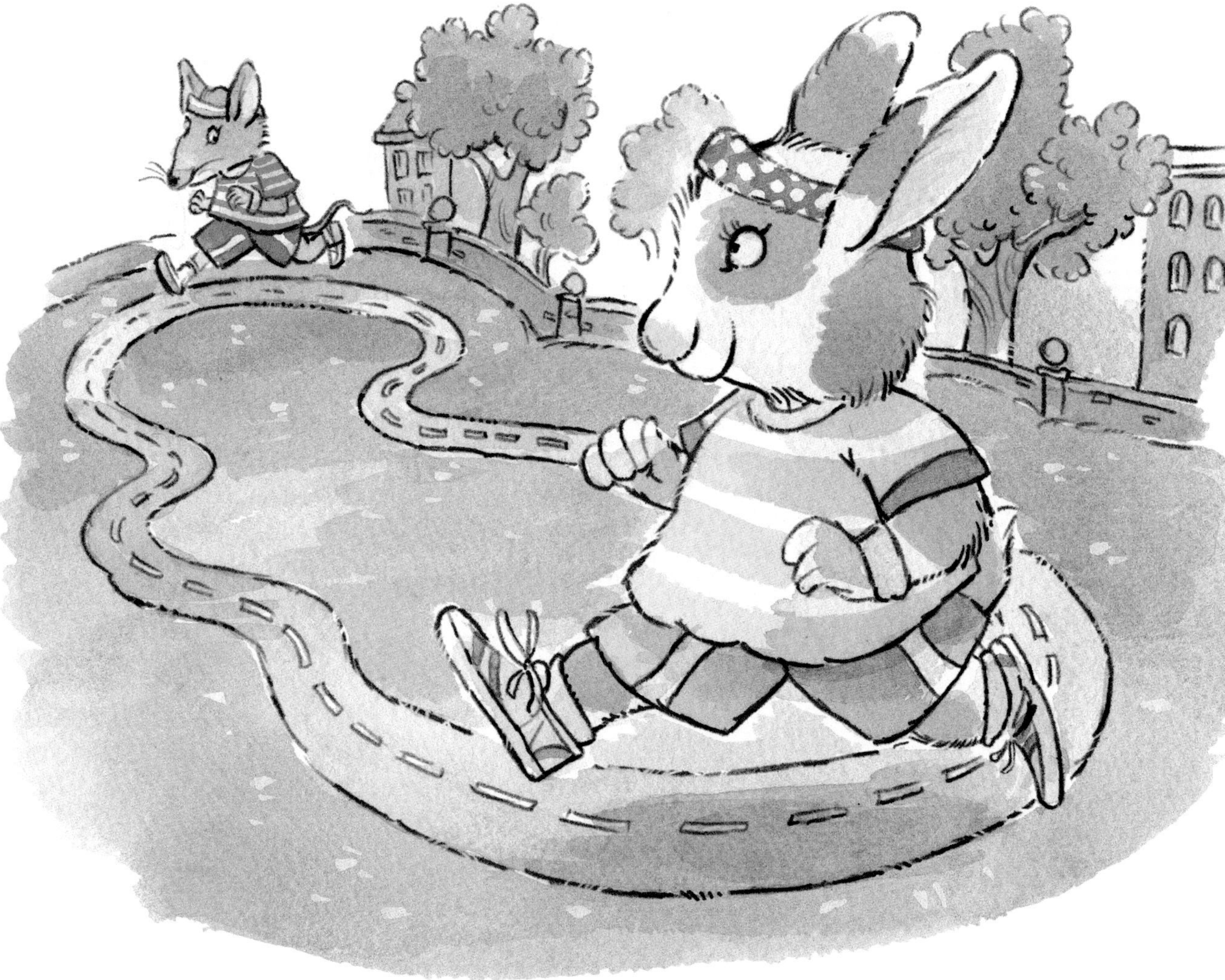

She ran!

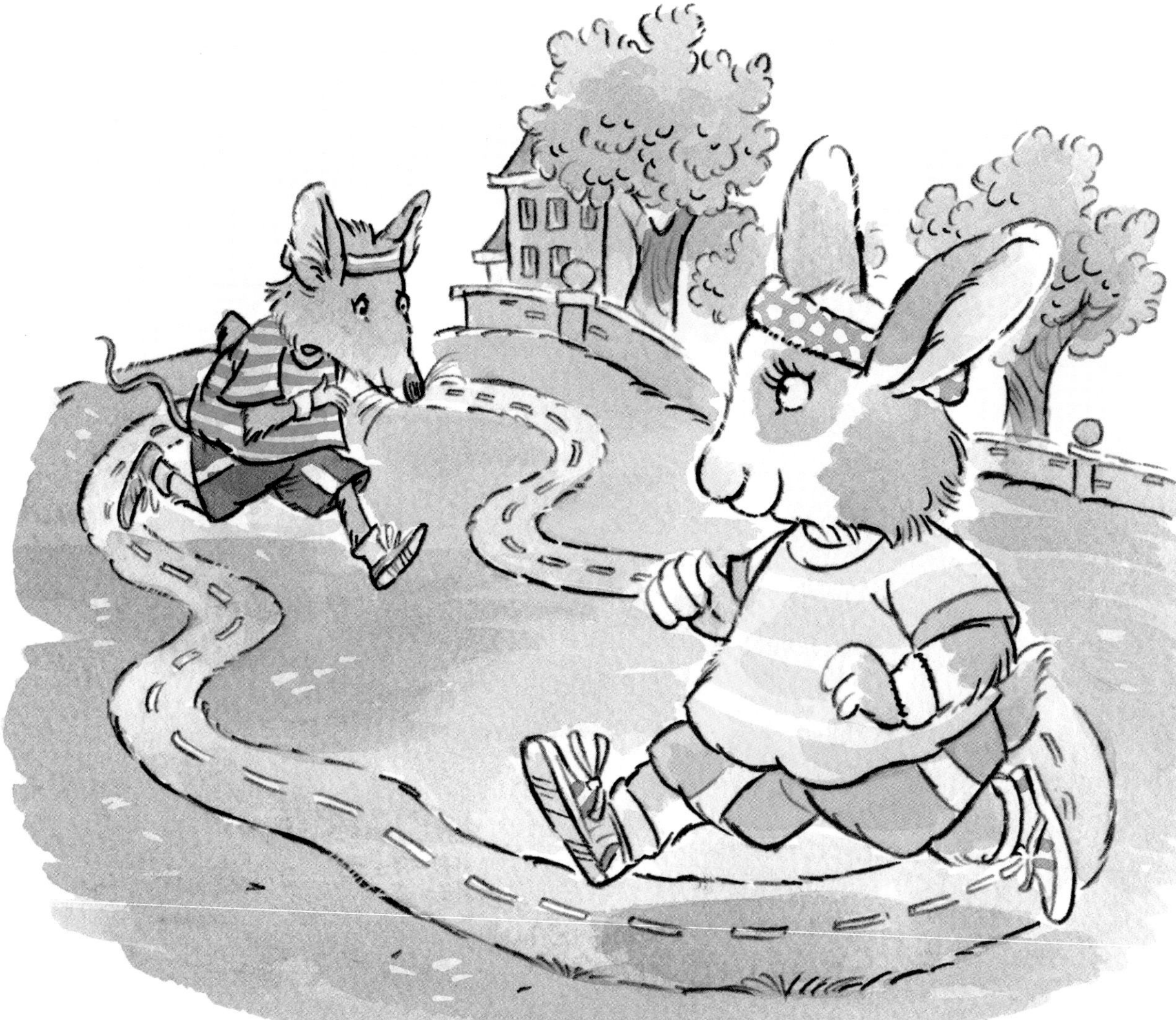

Ric ran and ran.

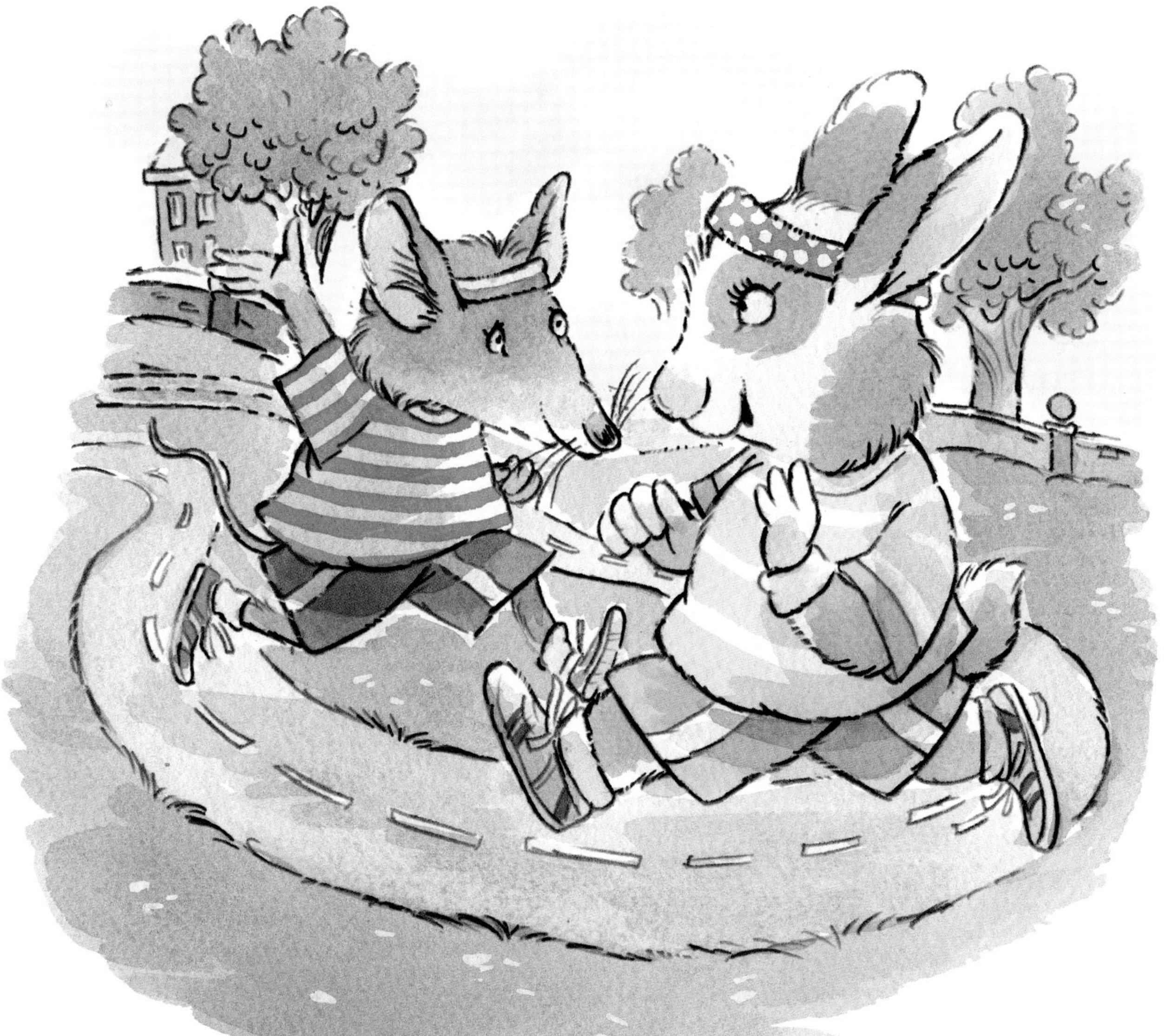

Rin ran and ran.

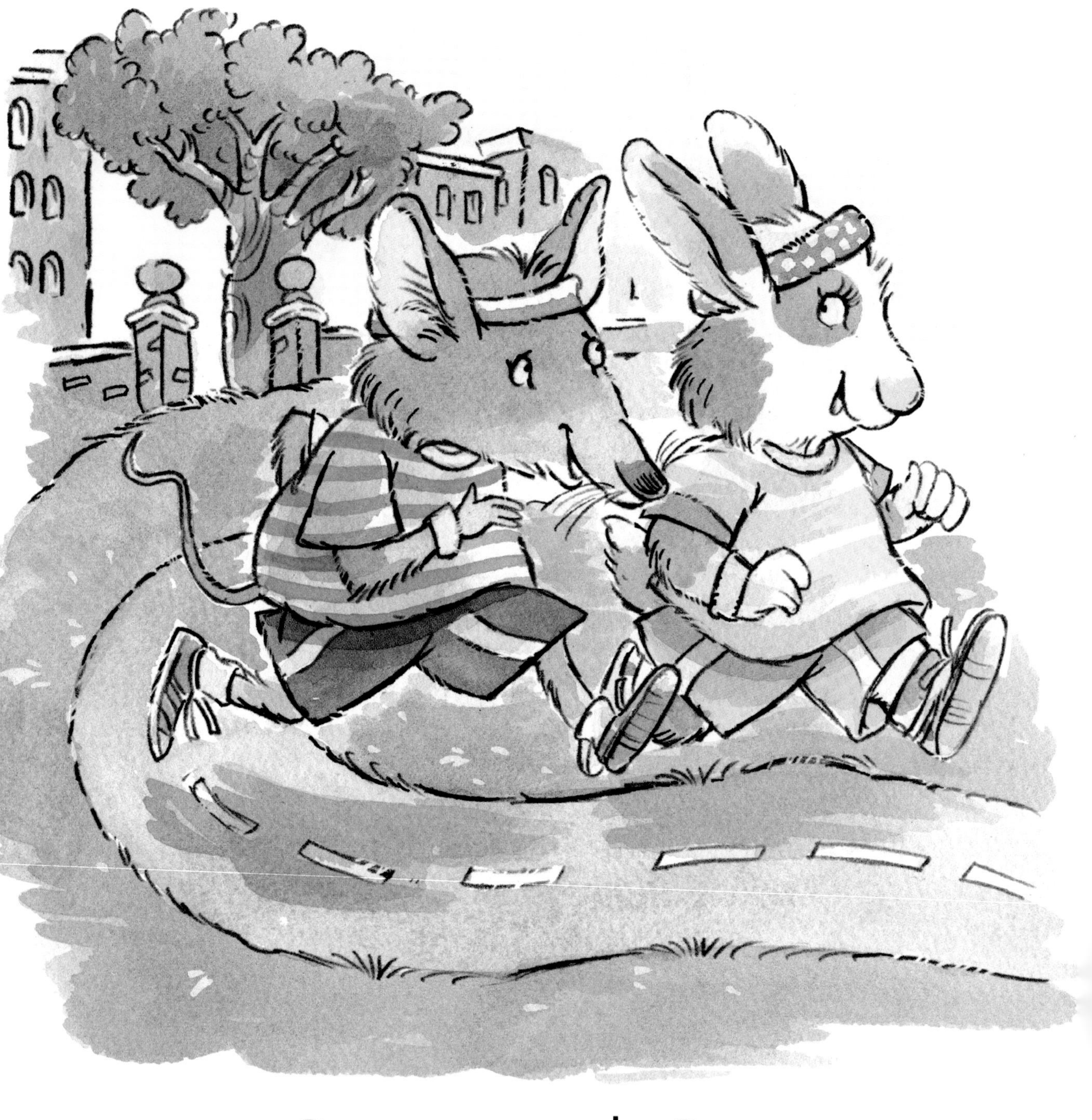

Ric ran with Rin.